Family Time

CONTENTS

 NATIONAL GEOGRAPHIC  Hampton-Brown

School Publishing

Sounds for m, s, h, t

Listen to the beginning sounds.

Example:

mouse

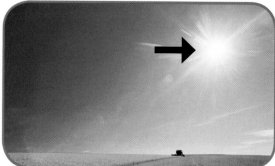

sun

sink

house

hat

table

High Frequency
Words

find
has
have
his
mother
too

Key Words

Look at the pictures.
Read the sentences.

Mother

1. I **have** a **mother**.
2. I like my mother.
3. Sam **has** a mother, **too**.
4. **Find** **his** mother.

His mother has a hat!

Phonics Games

NGReach.com

3

A Family

by Lada Kratky

I have a mother.

I have a mother, too.

I have a sister.

I have a sister, too.

I have a house.

I have a house, too.

I like my family. ❖

Sounds for m, s, h, t

Name each object in the picture. Listen to the sound at the beginning of each word. Point to the letter that makes the sound.

m	s	h	t

Talk Together

Talk about the picture. Then tell what sound you hear at the beginning of each thing you see.

I see <u>two</u> <u>sisters</u>.

11

Words with Short a

Look at each picture. Read the words.

a

Example:

h**a**t

m**a**t

S**a**m

s**a**t

12

High Frequency Words

find
has
his
have
mother
too

Key Words

Read the sentences. Match each sentence to one of the pictures.

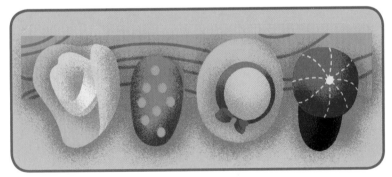

Hats

1. Sam **has** a hat.
2. **Find his** hat.
3. Find **Mother** a hat.
4. I **have** a hat, **too**.

My mother has a hat, too.

GO! **Phonics Games**

NGReach.com

Find a Hat

by Lada Kratky

illustrated by Jannie Ho

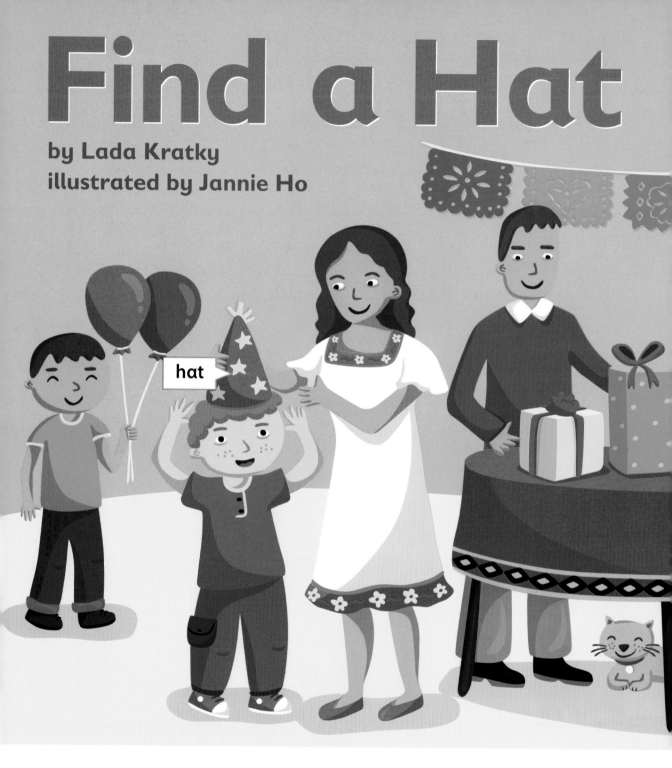

hat

Sam has a hat.

Find his hat.

Mat has a hat, too.

Find his hat.

Tam has a hat, too.

Find his hat.

Find Mother a hat! ❖

Words with Short <u>a</u>

Read these words.

am	ham	sat	Sam
at	hat	mat	

Use letters to build these words.

Talk Together

Choose words from the box above to tell your partner what you see in the picture.

I see a <u>hat</u>.

Find the Hats

Look at the pictures with a partner. Take turns reading the sentences. Then find the hat.

Find Sam.
Find his mother, too.
Find Sam a hat.

Find Mat.

Find his mother, too.

Find Pam.

Find Pam a hat.

Acknowledgments

Grateful acknowledgment is given to the authors, artists, photographers, museums, publishers, and agents for permission to reprint copyrighted material. Every effort has been made to secure the appropriate permission. If any omissions have been made or if corrections are required, please contact the Publisher.

Photographic Credits

CVR (Cover) Dean Mitchell/Shutterstock. **2** (bl) PhotoDisc/Getty Images. (br) Simon Krzic/ Shutterstock. (cl) Jacob Hellbach/iStockphoto. (cr) Susan Law Cain/Shutterstock. (tl) Sergey Lavrentev/iStockphoto. (tr) PhotoDisc/Getty Images. **3** (b) Liz Garza Williams/Hampton-Brown/National Geographic School Publishing. **4** (bl) mattasbestos/Shutterstock. (t) Mark Thiessen/Hampton-Brown/National Geographic School Publishing. **4-5** (bg) Charles Taylor/ Shutterstock. **5** (c) Mark Thiessen/Hampton-Brown/National Geographic School Publishing. (tl) (tr) (bl) mattasbestos/Shutterstock. **6** (c) Mark Thiessen/Hampton-Brown/National Geographic School Publishing. (tl) (br) mattasbestos/Shutterstock. **6-7** (bg) Charles Taylor/ Shutterstock. **7** (br) mattasbestos/Shutterstock. (t) Mark Thiessen/Hampton-Brown/National Geographic School Publishing. **8** (b) Mark Thiessen/Hampton-Brown/National Geographic School Publishing. (c) Daniel Deitschel/iStockphoto. (t) mattasbestos/Shutterstock. **8-9** (bg) Charles Taylor/Shutterstock. **9** (br) Mark Thiessen/Hampton-Brown/National Geographic School Publishing. (c) Jorge Salcedo/iStockphoto. (tr) (bl) mattasbestos/Shutterstock. **10** (bg) Charles Taylor/Shutterstock. (br) Mark Thiessen/Hampton-Brown/National Geographic School Publishing. (tl) Mark Thiessen/Hampton-Brown/National Geographic School Publishing. (tr) (bl) mattasbestos/Shutterstock. **11** (b) Liz Garza Williams/Hampton-Brown/National Geographic School Publishing. **12** (bl) Sean Locke/iStockphoto. (br) Blend Images/Veer. (tl) Dendong/ Shutterstock. (tr) R. Creation/amanaimages/Corbis. **13** (b) Liz Garza Williams/Hampton-Brown/National Geographic School Publishing. **21** (t) Liz Garza Williams/Hampton-Brown/ National Geographic School Publishing. **26** (cr) Mark Thiessen/Hampton-Brown/National Geographic School Publishing.

Illustrator Credits

3, 11, 13, 21, 22, 23 Paul Eric Roca; **14-20** Jannie Ho

The National Geographic Society

John M. Fahey, Jr., President & Chief Executive Officer
Gilbert M. Grosvenor, Chairman of the Board

National Geographic School Publishing
Hampton-Brown
www.NGSP.com

Printed in the USA.
RR Donnelley, Jefferson City, MO

ISBN:978-0-7362-8022-8

12 13 14 15 16 17 18 19
10 9 8 7 6 5 4